THE BEST 50
PICNIC FOODS

Bob Simmons
Coleen Simmons

BRISTOL PUBLISHING ENTERPRISES
San Leandro, California

Printed in the United States of America.

ISBN 1-55867-187-0

Cover design: Frank J. Paredes
Cover photography: John A. Benson
Food stylist: Susan Massey

LET'S HAVE A PICNIC!

Those words bring to mind pretty scenery, delicious food and enjoyable company. Picnic destinations can vary from your backyard or patio or a city park bench to the beach or a vineyard. Picnics are informal and fun. Food, whether simple or elaborate, always tastes better outdoors. The picnic basket can be an elegant straw hamper with matched plates, white table linens and crystal, a brown bag filled with deli goodies or a homemade sandwich on wholesome bread in your backpack.

NECESSITIES AND LUXURIES

Whatever the menu, an ice chest or insulated bag for keeping foods hot or cold, and plastic food containers with tight-fitting lids are basic picnic gear. If the occasion demands, include plates, glasses, eating utensils, salt and pepper, knife, small cutting board, napkins, picnic tablecloth or blanket, paper towels and bottled drinking water. Frequent picnickers may find it handy to keep a small picnic kit in the car trunk outfitted with these essentials, and perhaps a can opener and corkscrew.

PACKING YOUR PICNIC FOODS

It is important to safeguard picnic foods. Small frozen ice packs provide cooling without dripping. Keep foods as cold as possible before packing. Pack perishable chicken, fish, meat or dairy products close to the ice source. Salads, whether they have a mayonnaise dressing or not, benefit from being kept cool and stay refreshingly crisp. At the picnic site, place ice chests and food in the cool shade. If it is very sunny and hot, consider putting out food in courses, or serving only a small portion at a time while you keep the remainder cool.

A little organization while packing the food makes the picnic more carefree. Pack by courses and keep the course items together. The salads should be grouped with associated dressings, parsley, crackers or go-withs. Green salads should always be tossed at the last minute, so carry the dressing in a separate container with a tight-fitting lid. If you are taking a whole cold roast chicken or a roast beef, you may want to carve it at home and reform it in a large plastic container, or wrap up individual pieces in plastic wrap or foil. Square containers take up less space than round ones, and some attractive containers can double as serving dishes. Pies and cakes, after cooling, can be wrapped in foil or plastic wrap and placed back in the baking pan. Layer the foods in the picnic basket or ice chest so the first items to be served are on top.

RULE #1: ENJOY IT!

Sometimes the best picnics are impromptu, needing only a quick stop at the market or delicatessen to pick up ready-to-eat items. If you have the time and interest, however, it is fun to cook something delicious for a picnic. Or just make one dish and buy the rest of the food. It is more important to enjoy the planning and eating than to cook for days ahead of time. *The Best 50 Picnic Foods* includes a variety of choices to prepare at home that don't require further cooking when you get to the picnic site. There are tasty vegetable and fish salads, hearty entrées and finger foods. Patés, handpies, cold chicken, deviled eggs and sandwiches are also popular picnic fare. Some luscious desserts round out the picnic basket.

Picnics are for sharing food and fun, so invite a special friend or two to come along.

COLD STUFFED ARTICHOKES

Cooked artichokes are great picnic fare. Stuff them with a shrimp, ham or chicken salad mixture, or serve them plain with a little mayonnaise.

FOR EACH MEDIUM ARTICHOKE
1 tbs. mayonnaise
1 tbs. sour cream
1 tsp. Dijon mustard
2 tbs. chopped cooked chicken, ham or shrimp
2 tsp. diced celery or walnuts
salt and freshly ground pepper to taste

Wash artichoke, cut off stem and remove top ¼ by cutting straight across top. Pull off 2 to 3 layers of outer leaves. Trim rough edges of artichoke bottom where leaves were removed. Place on a rack and steam artichoke upside down for 30 to 35 minutes until bottom is tender when pierced with a knife. Drain and let cool, or cook ahead and refrigerate until ready to use. Scoop out the inedible hairy choke and discard. Combine mayonnaise, sour cream, mustard, chicken, celery, salt and pepper and spoon into center of artichoke.

Makes 1 serving

MARINATED SHRIMP

Eat as is, or pair some of these mildly piquant shrimp with a salad. They can be made a day ahead.

½ lb. medium shrimp, peeled
   and deveined
1 tbs. chopped fresh parsley
1 tbs. full-flavored olive oil
1 tbs. tarragon wine vinegar

1 tbs. lemon juice
1 tsp. Dijon mustard
3-4 drops Tabasco Sauce
2 small green onions, minced
salt and freshly ground pepper

Cook shrimp in boiling salted water for about 1 minute or until they turn pink and are firm. Drain well. Combine remaining ingredients and pour over shrimp while still warm. Mix well. Cover and refrigerate for 3 to 4 hours before serving.

Makes 3-4 servings

DEVILED EGGS

What is a picnic without deviled eggs? Be creative! Add these combinations to cooked egg yolks and stuff cooked egg white halves.

- smoked salmon, dill weed and mayonnaise

- sardines, mustard and mayonnaise

- pesto and cream cheese

- olive paste and sour cream

- cooked shrimp or chicken with curry powder, chutney and sour cream

- stuffed green olives and mayonnaise

- prepared salsa, hot or mild, and sour cream

- cooked mushrooms, tarragon and sour cream

- ham with dill pickle, mustard and mayonnaise

- capers, pine nuts and mayonnaise

MARINATED CARROT STICKS

Low calorie, slightly crunchy, these will keep for about 1 week.

2 large cloves garlic, smashed
2 tbs. olive oil
3 large carrots, about ½ lb., cut
  into matchstick pieces

1 tbs. red wine vinegar
¼ tsp. dried oregano
salt and freshly ground pepper

In a small skillet, sauté garlic in olive oil over low heat for 2 to 3 minutes until lightly browned. Discard garlic and reserve oil.

In a saucepan, boil carrots in water for 3 to 4 minutes, until crisp-tender. Drain and rinse with cold water. Place in a bowl and, while still warm, toss with remaining ingredients. Cover and store in the refrigerator. Shake bowl to distribute marinade from time to time.

Makes 4-6 servings

OVEN-ROASTED ASPARAGUS IN HAM

Ham-wrapped asparagus spears are easy to pack and easy to eat.

1 lb. thick fresh asparagus	lemon juice
1 tbs. full-flavored olive oil	5-6 thin slices Danish ham
salt and freshly ground pepper	1-2 tbs. Dijon mustard

Heat oven to 400°. Wash asparagus, break off tough ends and pat dry. Line a 9-x-13-inch baking pan with foil; sprinkle foil with olive oil, salt and pepper. Roll asparagus spears over foil to coat with oil. Roast for 10 minutes, turn spears over and continue to roast until spears are tender when pierced. Remove from oven, sprinkle with a few drops of lemon juice and let cool slightly. Spread ham slices with mustard on one side and cut each piece into thirds. Spiral-wrap one piece, mustard-side in, around each asparagus spear.

Makes about 15

MARINATED MUSHROOMS

These zesty, low-calorie mushrooms keep well for a week.

1/4 cup olive oil
1 large clove garlic, smashed
1/4 cup rice vinegar
1/8 tsp. red pepper flakes
1 tbs. lemon juice

1/4 tsp. sugar
1/2 tsp. dried thyme
1/2 tsp. dried basil
salt and freshly ground pepper
1/2 lb. small button mushrooms

In a saucepan, bring all ingredients, except mushrooms, to a boil. Reduce heat and simmer for 5 minutes. Trim mushroom stems. Leave small mushrooms whole; cut larger mushrooms in halves or quarters. Add to saucepan and simmer for 5 minutes, stirring once or twice. Remove from heat and cool mushrooms in liquid. Store in liquid in a small tightly covered jar in the refrigerator.

Makes 1 1/2 cups

SPICY CHICKEN-STUFFED SHELLS

These go together very quickly if you have leftover chicken.

8 jumbo pasta shells, cooked
2 oz. light cream cheese
1/4 cup prepared chunky salsa,
    hot or mild to taste
salt and freshly ground pepper

1 tbs. chopped fresh cilantro
2 tbs. coarsely chopped almonds
1 cup cooked diced chicken
fresh cilantro leaves for garnish

Drain and rinse cooked shells under cold water. Set aside while preparing filling. In a medium bowl, combine cream cheese, salsa, salt and pepper, chopped cilantro and almonds. Mix well. Add chicken pieces and mix well. Stuff cooked pasta shells with chicken mixture and garnish each shell with a fresh whole cilantro leaf. Refrigerate. Remove from ice chest about 15 minutes before serving for best flavor.

Makes 8

DOLMAS

Stuffed grape leaves make great picnic finger food and keep well in the refrigerator for several days.

½ cup olive oil, plus 1 tbs.
1 large onion, chopped
1 clove garlic, minced
salt and freshly ground pepper
½ cup uncooked long-grain rice
½ tsp. dried dill weed
3 tbs. minced fresh parsley
2 tbs. chopped almonds or pine
    nuts

2 tbs. lemon juice
½ cup water or chicken stock
½ lb. fresh button mushrooms,
    finely chopped
1 jar (8 oz.) grape leaves in brine
¼ cup lemon juice
1½ cups water or chicken stock

Heat ¼ cup of the olive oil in large skillet. Add onion and garlic; sauté for 6 to 8 minutes until soft. Add salt, pepper and rice to onion and cook slowly for 10 minutes, stirring frequently. Add dill, parsley, nuts, 2 tbs. lemon juice and water. Stir well. Cover and simmer gently until liquid has been absorbed, about 15 to 20 minutes. Heat 3 tbs. olive oil in a small skillet. Sauté mushrooms for 3 to 4 minutes until mixture is fairly dry. Add to rice mixture after rice has cooked.

Rinse grape leaves under running water. Separate and trim long stems even with base of leaves. Place leaves shiny-side down on a plate or board. To fill, place 1 tsp. of rice-mushroom mixture near stem edge and roll up jelly roll-style, tucking in sides of leaves as you roll.

Place stuffed leaves seam-side down in a skillet large enough to hold them in one layer. Combine remaining 2 tbs. olive oil with lemon juice and water or chicken stock and pour into skillet. Liquid should come halfway up sides of dolmas. Place a large flat lid or plate directly on top of rolls. Cover pan with foil or another lid. Simmer for 35 minutes. Add more water during cooking if necessary. Transfer to a platter and cool.

Makes 25-30

HUMMUS BI TAHINI

*Use crisp raw vegetable pieces or **Crisp Pita Chips**, page 15, to scoop up this popular Middle Eastern dip. Good vegetable dippers include raw carrots, snow peas, zucchini, cucumber, bell peppers, fennel, jicama and turnips.*

2 cloves garlic
1 can (15½ oz.) garbanzo beans
¼ cup tahini or Oriental sesame paste
1 tbs. full-flavored olive oil
¼ cup lemon juice
1 tsp. ground cumin
salt and white pepper
paprika, fresh cilantro and black olives or
cherry tomato halves for garnish

Using a food processor with the motor running, drop garlic cloves into feed tube of workbowl. Drain garbanzo beans, reserving about 3 tbs. of the liquid. Place garbanzo beans in workbowl with 2 tbs. of the liquid, sesame paste, olive oil and lemon juice. Process until smooth. Scrape down container sides and add cumin, salt and pepper. Process for another few seconds to mix. If mixture seems too thick to dip, add remaining 1 tbs. garbanzo liquid. Pour into a serving container or dish and sprinkle lightly with paprika. Refrigerate or set in a cool place for 1 to 2 hours to allow flavors to develop. Garnish with fresh cilantro leaves and black olives or cherry tomato halves. This keeps well for several days in the refrigerator.

Makes 1¾ cups

CRISP PITA CHIPS

Heat oven to 225°. Cut each pita bread into 8 wedges, separate wedges into 2 halves and place triangles on a baking sheet, rough-side up. Bake for about 30 minutes until crisp and dry, but not brown. Let cool and store in an airtight container. Use with dips or spreads.

MEDITERRANEAN SALAD

Classic Mediterranean ingredients are combined to make an irresistible salad. Eat it with a fork, roll it in crisp lettuce leaves and eat it out of hand or use it to stuff a pita pocket. The microwave does a great job of cooking the eggplant with very little oil.

½ lb. small eggplant
1 tbs. full-flavored olive oil
1 large clove garlic, minced
¼ tsp. dried thyme, or leaves from a few fresh sprigs
6-8 black Greek or Italian olives, coarsely chopped
2 oz. crumbled feta cheese
2 tbs. diced red onion
¼ cup chopped roasted red pepper
1 tbs. minced fresh parsley

1 tbs. lemon juice
salt and freshly ground pepper

Cut unpeeled eggplant into ½-inch cubes. Place in a microwave dish with olive oil, garlic and thyme. Cover and cook on HIGH for 3 minutes. Stir, cover and cook for 2 minutes. Let stand for a few minutes before using. In a medium bowl, combine remaining ingredients and cooked eggplant. Refrigerate for 1 to 2 hours before serving.

Makes 2 servings

TUSCAN BEAN SALAD

This hearty salad is easy to put together from pantry ingredients. It's good garnished with chopped fresh tomato.

1 can (6½ oz.) tuna, drained
2 tbs. finely diced celery
2 tbs. finely diced red onion
2 tbs. chopped fresh parsley
1 small clove garlic, minced
2 tbs. full-flavored olive oil

2 tbs. red wine vinegar
1 tbs. lemon juice
1 drop Tabasco Sauce
salt and freshly ground pepper
1 can (15 oz.) cannellini beans,
   rinsed and drained

In a large bowl, place all ingredients, except beans. Stir with a fork to combine, breaking up tuna pieces. Add beans and mix gently. If possible, refrigerate for at least 1 to 2 hours before serving to allow flavors to blend.

Makes 4 servings

SOUTHWESTERN SALAD

This hearty salad has South-of-the-Border flavor.

1 can (15½ oz.) pinto beans
1 can (11 oz.) corn
1 cup diced cooked potatoes
4-5 green onions, finely chopped
4-5 tbs. finely chopped canned
    green chiles
½ tsp. chili powder

1 tsp. dried oregano
1 tsp. Dijon mustard
1 tbs. lemon juice
¼ cup mayonnaise
¼ cup sour cream
2 tbs. minced fresh parsley
salt and freshly ground pepper

Rinse and drain beans and corn. In a large bowl, using 2 forks, gently combine all ingredients. Chill in the refrigerator for 2 hours before serving. This salad will keep for 2 to 3 days in the refrigerator.

Makes 6-8 servings

COLD SHRIMP AND NOODLE SALAD

Use thin Japanese- or Chinese-style noodles for this elegant salad. If you have medium shrimp, cut them in half lengthwise and cut the vegetables in thin strips about same diameter as the noodles. A lemon zester makes beautiful, long, thin carrot strips for this salad. For an interesting variation, add a few bean sprouts and thin strips of fresh red or green bell pepper.

8 oz. fresh thin Oriental-style noodles, or 6 oz. dried noodles
2 tbs. peanut oil
8 oz. cooked medium shrimp or small salad shrimp
2 tbs. rice vinegar or cider vinegar
1 tsp. dark sesame oil
1 tbs. light soy sauce
3-4 drops Tabasco Sauce

1 small carrot, coarsely grated or cut into very thin strips
6-8 snow peas, blanched for 1 minute, cut into thin strips
3 green onions, white part only, cut into thin strips
salt and freshly ground pepper

Marinate shrimp in a small bowl with rice vinegar, sesame oil, soy sauce and Tabasco while cooking noodles. Cook noodles according to package directions. Rinse under cold water and drain. Place in a large bowl and toss with peanut oil. Add shrimp, carrot strips, snow peas, green onions, salt and pepper to noodles. Toss with 2 forks. Chill for 1 hour in the refrigerator before serving.

Makes 6 servings

Note: To blanch snow peas, lower into boiling water for 1 minute and immediately submerge in cold water to stop the cooking process.

CONFETTI PASTA SALAD

Crisp bits of fresh vegetables and cooked chicken make this a light, pretty salad that can be served all year long. Salad shrimp or ham chunks could be substituted for chicken.

4 oz. dried corkscrew pasta
¼ cup full-flavored olive oil
1 cup diced cooked chicken
3 green onions, thinly sliced
½ medium red or green bell pepper, diced
1 small carrot, coarsely grated
4-5 black olives, sliced
1 tbs. minced fresh basil, or 1 tsp. dried
2 tbs. grated Parmesan cheese

dash red pepper flakes
1 tsp. Dijon mustard
1 tbs. white wine vinegar
1 tsp. lemon juice
salt and freshly ground pepper

Cook pasta according to package directions. Drain and rinse with cold water. Toss in a large bowl with 1 tbs. of the olive oil. Set aside to cool. To cooled pasta, add chicken, onions, diced pepper, carrot, olives, basil, Parmesan cheese and red pepper flakes. In a small bowl, combine mustard, remaining olive oil, vinegar and lemon juice. Whisk to form an emulsion. Pour over pasta and vegetables and mix with 2 forks. Taste for seasoning and add salt and pepper to taste. Pack in ice chest; remove about 20 minutes before serving.

Makes 4-6 servings

CHINESE-STYLE CHICKEN SALAD

Pack the lettuce, grated carrot and green onions in one plastic container and the marinated chicken in another. Combine them when you are ready to eat.

1 cup shredded or thinly sliced cooked chicken
1 tbs. soy sauce
1 tbs. rice vinegar
1 tbs. peanut oil
1 tsp. dark sesame oil
2 tsp. Dijon mustard
dash red pepper flakes
$1/4$ tsp. sugar
salt and freshly ground pepper

1-1½ cups shredded iceberg lettuce
1 cup coarsely grated carrots
2 green onions, thinly sliced
2 tbs. chopped dry-roasted unsalted peanuts
fresh cilantro leaves for garnish

Combine shredded chicken, soy sauce, rice vinegar, peanut oil, sesame oil, mustard, red pepper flakes, sugar, salt and pepper in a small bowl or plastic bag. Marinate for several hours in the refrigerator. Drain chicken, reserving marinade.

To assemble, place lettuce and carrots on a plate or platter. Sprinkle with green onion slices. Mound chicken in the center of salad, drizzle with marinade and garnish with peanuts and fresh cilantro leaves.

Makes 2 servings

ORANGE AND FENNEL SALAD

Thinly sliced oranges, some crunchy fennel and a dash of cumin make a very refreshing salad. Black olives make a striking garnish.

2 small oranges, or 1 large
one 2-inch piece fennel bulb,
   cut into thin strips
1 green onion, thinly sliced

$1/8$ tsp. ground cumin
$1/2$ tsp. light olive oil
freshly ground pepper
$1/4$ tsp. sugar, optional

Place 1 orange on a cutting board. With a small, sharp knife, remove peel and as much of the white membrane as possible. When peeled, cut into very thin slices and place in a small bowl. Add fennel, green onion, cumin, olive oil and pepper. If oranges are quite sour, add sugar. Cover and marinate in the refrigerator for 1 to 2 hours before serving.

Makes 2 servings

SMOKED SALMON AND
DILLED POTATO SALAD

New potatoes in their jackets and just a little smoked salmon make an elegantly different picnic salad.

1 tbs. sweet hot mustard
1-2 tbs. sour cream
2 tsp. chopped fresh dill, or
    ¼ tsp. dried
1 tsp. minced fresh parsley

¾ lb. small new potatoes,
    cooked, quartered
salt and freshly ground pepper
1-2 oz. smoked salmon, cut
    into 1-inch squares

In a bowl, mix together mustard, sour cream, dill and parsley. Add potatoes and toss gently. Season with salt and pepper. Add salmon and mix gently. Refrigerate until ready to serve.

Makes 4 servings

COUSCOUS SALAD

Couscous, also called Moroccan pasta, is paired with some colorful fresh crunchy vegetables.

¾ cup water
1 tbs. olive oil
½ cup quick-cooking couscous
¼ cup diced cucumber
¼ cup coarsely grated carrot
3-4 radishes, finely chopped
1 tbs. finely chopped red onion
2 tbs. finely chopped green bell pepper
1 small tomato, peeled, seeded, chopped
2-3 black olives, chopped

1 tsp. capers
1 tbs. chopped fresh Italian parsley
salt and freshly ground pepper
1 tbs. full-flavored olive oil
2 tsp. balsamic vinegar

Bring water and 1 tbs. olive oil to a boil in a small saucepan. Add couscous, stir, cover and remove from heat. Let stand for 5 minutes and then fluff with a fork. Set aside to cool.

Place couscous in a medium bowl. Add chopped vegetables, olives, capers, parsley, salt, pepper, 1 tbs. olive oil and balsamic vinegar. Use 2 forks to combine ingredients. Cover and refrigerate for several hours. This keeps well for 3 or 4 days in the refrigerator.

Makes 2-3 servings

VARIATION
Serve in tomato or bell pepper cups.

COLD MEXICAN FISH SALAD

Serve this cooked seviche in a lettuce cup with some crisp tortilla chips or crackers.

salt and pepper
1/2 lb. fresh sole, snapper or other thin fillets
flour for dredging
3 tbs. vegetable oil
1 tbs. lemon juice
1 tbs. lime juice
1 tbs. chopped canned green chiles
1 tbs. chopped roasted red bell pepper or pimiento
1 tsp. Tabasco Jalapeño Sauce
2 tsp. olive oil

½ tsp. dried oregano
salt and freshly ground pepper
1 small avocado, diced
1 small tomato, peeled, seeded and chopped
fresh cilantro leaves for garnish
4 large iceberg lettuce leaves

Salt and pepper fish and lightly dust with flour. Heat vegetable oil in a skillet over medium-high heat and sauté fish for 3 to 4 minutes each side until cooked through. Place on a paper towel-lined platter and let cool slightly before cutting into ½- to ¾-inch pieces. Place fish in a glass or stainless steel pan or bowl and sprinkle with lemon and lime juice. Add green chiles, roasted red pepper, Tabasco Jalapeño Sauce, olive oil, oregano, salt and pepper; toss together gently. Cover and refrigerate for at least 1 hour. When ready to serve, combine fish with avocado, tomato and cilantro leaves and serve in lettuce leaves.

Makes 4 servings

HONEY-GLAZED CHICKEN LEGS

This is an easy baked chicken recipe using garlic, ginger and honey to give the chicken pieces a little lift. It's delicious served warm or cold.

12 chicken legs, skin and excess fat removed
1/2 cup soy sauce
1/3 cup honey
2 tbs. vegetable oil
1 clove garlic, minced
1 tsp. grated ginger root

Place chicken legs in a food storage bag. Combine remaining ingredients and pour over chicken. Seal bag and refrigerate for several hours or overnight, turning bag occasionally so all pieces of chicken are covered by marinade.

Heat oven to 375°. Line a rimmed baking sheet with foil. Remove chicken pieces from marinade and place on foil. Discard marinade. Bake for 25 minutes. Turn chicken pieces over and increase oven temperature to 400°. Continue to bake for about 20 minutes until chicken is cooked through. Transfer to a plate and cool slightly before refrigerating.

Makes 6 servings

ORANGE-GLAZED CORNISH GAME HENS

Golden brown game hens are perfect picnic fare. If you plan to serve each person a half hen, you can divide the roasted hens at home, or take along a pair of kitchen shears to cut them easily.

2 Cornish game hens, about 1½ lb. each
2 quarter-sized pieces ginger root, unpeeled
2 cloves garlic, smashed
2 tbs. vegetable oil
salt and freshly ground pepper
2 tbs. soy sauce
2 tbs. frozen orange juice concentrate, thawed
1 tbs. cider vinegar
a few drops Tabasco Sauce

Heat oven to 400°. Remove giblets from hens and discard. Wash and dry hens and place a piece of ginger and 1 clove garlic in each cavity. Truss hens, rub each with 1 tbs. of the vegetable oil and sprinkle with salt and pepper.

Place on an oiled rack in a baking pan breast-side down. Combine remaining oil with remaining ingredients, brush backs with marinade and bake for 20 minutes. After 20 minutes, turn hens breast-side up. Continue to baste every 10 to 15 minutes until an instant-read thermometer inserted into the inner thigh reads 175° and hens are nicely browned, about 45 to 55 minutes. Cool and refrigerate. Pack in an ice chest and keep cool until ready to serve.

Makes 2-4 servings

COLD ROAST BEEF WITH CAPER SAUCE

This is a great picnic dish. The roast beef is also delicious made into a sandwich with rye bread and some strong mustard.

2½-3 lb. eye of round roast, well trimmed
1 tbs. olive oil
salt and freshly ground pepper
½ tsp. dried thyme
Caper Sauce, follows

Heat oven to 400°. Rub beef with olive oil, salt, pepper and thyme. Place in a roasting pan and roast for about 50 minutes, or until internal temperature reaches 135° to 140°. Remove from oven and cool for 1 hour before refrigerating. Meat can be thinly sliced and arranged on a platter, covered and refrigerated. Keep meat and sauce cool in an ice chest until ready to serve. Lightly coat slices with sauce or pass sauce separately.

Makes 8-10 servings

CAPER SAUCE

½ cup mayonnaise
½ cup sour cream
1 tbs. Dijon mustard
½ tsp. prepared horseradish
2 tsp. lemon juice
3 tbs. coarsely chopped capers
2 tsp. finely chopped fresh chives
salt and freshly ground pepper

Combine ingredients. Cover and refrigerate.

Makes about 1⅓ cups

SPANISH POTATO OMELET

Wedges of this classic Spanish midmorning snack travel well.

3 tbs. olive oil
1 small onion, thinly sliced
2 cups quartered, thinly sliced cooked boiling potatoes
4 eggs
3 tbs. chopped fresh parsley
salt and freshly ground pepper to taste

Heat oven to 325°. In a 10-inch nonstick skillet with an ovenproof handle, heat olive oil and sauté onion for 4 to 5 minutes until it starts to soften. Add potato slices, stir to coat slices with oil and cook over very low heat for about 10 minutes.

Beat eggs with 2 tbs. of the parsley in a small bowl. Pour over potatoes and onion, gently lifting potatoes to distribute eggs evenly. Cook uncovered over low heat until eggs set on the bottom of skillet. Place in oven and bake for about 5 to 8 minutes until top is set. Turn out on a large plate and cool. Remove from ice chest a few minutes before serving. Cut into wedges and sprinkle with parsley.

Makes 4 servings

COLD POACHED SALMON STEAKS

*Cold poached salmon makes elegant picnic fare. Serve with **Caper Sauce**, page 37, and a crisp white wine.*

3 cups water
1 cup dry white wine
1 lemon, thinly sliced
1 small onion, thinly sliced
2-3 sprigs fresh parsley
1 tsp. salt
4-6 salmon steaks, about 1-inch thick
lettuce leaves
Caper Sauce

Combine water, wine, lemon, onion slices, parsley and salt in a skillet large enough to hold fish in a single layer. Bring to a boil, reduce heat and simmer for 10 minutes. Carefully place salmon steaks in hot liquid and cook over low heat for about 10 minutes, or until fish is firm to the touch. Using a wide spatula, transfer fish from liquid to a large platter. Cool. Remove skin and bones, keeping fish in pieces as large as possible. Refrigerate salmon. When ready to serve, arrange lettuce leaves on a serving plate; top with salmon fillets. Spoon a little *Caper Sauce* over each piece of fish.

Makes 4-6 servings

TURKEY MOSAIC TERRINE

Grated apple gives this terrine a light, moist texture without adding extra fat. For a different look, substitute diced red bell peppers, black olives and green beans for the apple, carrots and peas.

⅓ cup chopped onion
1 small clove garlic, minced
2 tbs. peanut oil
1 lb. ground turkey meat
1 tart apple, peeled, coarsely
    grated
1 tbs. Worcestershire sauce

1 tbs. Dijon mustard
¼ tsp. dried tarragon or basil
1 egg, beaten
⅓ cup diced cooked carrots
⅓ cup frozen peas
salt and freshly ground pepper

Heat oven to 350°. Sauté onion in oil until soft and translucent, about 4 to 5 minutes. Add garlic and cook 1 minute. Cool before adding to turkey mixture. Place turkey in a large bowl. Add apple, Worcestershire, mustard, tarragon, egg, onion and garlic. Mix well. Stir in carrots, peas, salt and pepper.

Oil a 4-cup baking mold or small loaf pan. Fill mold with meat mixture. Cover with foil and place in a larger baking pan. Fill larger pan with very hot water to come ¾ up sides of baking mold. After baking for 30 minutes, remove foil cover and continue to bake for another 30 to 45 minutes until internal temperature of terrine reaches 170°.

Remove from oven. Pour off excess liquid from terrine and place mold on a rack. Cover meat with a small piece of foil and weight down with a heavy can until cool. Refrigerate for several hours before serving. Cut into ½- to ¾-inch slices to serve.

Makes 12-14 slices

HAM AND APPLE PATÉ

Applesauce lightens this savory paté, made with ham, apple and dried cranberries.

6 slices bacon
½ cup dried cranberries or
    dried cherries
¼ cup brandy
1¾ lb. ground pork
1 cup applesauce
2 eggs
½ cup heavy cream
1 clove garlic, finely chopped
1½ tsp. salt

¼ tsp. nutmeg
¼ tsp. allspice
½ tsp. dry mustard
pinch cloves
freshly ground pepper
2 Golden Delicious apples,
    peeled, cut into ½-inch chunks
6 oz. sliced smoked ham, cut
    into ⅜-inch cubes

Heat oven to 350°. Line the bottom of an 8-cup loaf pan with 3 strips of the bacon and set aside. Place a large pan in the oven, filled with enough hot water to come halfway up sides of loaf pan. In a small bowl, soak cranberries in brandy. In a food processor or mixer bowl, combine pork, applesauce, eggs and cream. Process until well blended. Drain brandy from cranberries and add to meat mixture with garlic and spices. Mix well. Stir in apple pieces.

Spread about 1/3 of the meat mixture in loaf pan and scatter 1/2 of the ham cubes and 1/2 of the cranberries evenly over meat. Top with another 1/3 of the meat mixture, remaining ham and cranberries. Finish with remaining meat. Place 3 remaining bacon slices over top of paté, cover tightly with foil and place in water bath in oven. Bake for about 1 hour and 45 minutes, to an internal temperature of 160°. Uncover for last 15 minutes of baking.

Remove paté from oven and carefully pour off juices. Cover paté with a piece of foil and weight down with some heavy cans. Cool to room temperature; refrigerate. Unmold and cut into 1/2-inch slices to serve.

Makes 12-14 slices

MUSHROOM PATÉ

Use the food processor to chop the onions, garlic, mushrooms and parsley. This intensely flavored paté is delicious by itself or makes a great sandwich with lettuce and Dijon mustard.

1/2 oz. dried porcini or shiitake
    mushrooms
hot water to cover
1/4 cup olive oil
1 large onion, finely chopped
1 lb. fresh button mushrooms,
    finely chopped
2 cloves garlic, minced
dash red pepper flakes
2 eggs, lightly beaten

1/2 cup cracker crumbs
2 tbs. diced roasted red bell
    pepper
2 tbs. grated Parmesan cheese
2 tbs. finely chopped fresh
    parsley
1/2 tsp. dried basil
1/2 tsp. dried oregano
salt and freshly ground pepper

Heat oven to 350°. Cover dried mushrooms with hot water and soak for 20 minutes to soften. Remove, squeeze dry and chop coarsely. In a large skillet, heat oil over high heat and sauté onion, fresh mushrooms, garlic and red pepper flakes for 5 to 6 minutes until all liquid has evaporated and mixture is dry, but not brown. Cool for a few minutes. Combine mushroom mixture, dried mushrooms, eggs, cracker crumbs, red peppers and remaining ingredients in skillet; mix well.

Lightly oil a 4-cup mold or loaf pan. Place a strip of foil in pan to cover bottom of pan and come partially up the sides; this will help when removing paté from pan. Pour mushroom mixture into pan and bake for about 1 hour, or until paté is firm and lightly browned. Cool to room temperature before covering and refrigerating. To serve, unmold and cut into ½-inch slices. This keeps well for 3 or 4 days.

Makes 10 slices

MARINATED GOAT CHEESE

*Although not a paté, this cheese can be eaten in the same way —
on bread or crackers, or by itself. Cheese is a welcome addition to a
picnic basket. Make this a few hours ahead.*

3 tbs. full-flavored olive oil
8-10 cloves garlic, peeled
1 log (11 oz.) fresh goat cheese, about 2-inch diameter
1/4 tsp. red pepper flakes
1/2 cup slivered sun-dried tomatoes, oil-packed
1 tsp. dried rosemary, oregano or herbes de Provence
1 tbs. capers, rinsed and drained
freshly ground pepper

Heat 2 tbs. of the olive oil in a small skillet. Sauté garlic cloves over low heat until lightly browned and soft. Watch carefully so they do not burn. Remove from heat and set aside to cool. Slice goat cheese log into 8 to 10 slices and place slices in a single layer in a shallow portable container or deep-sided plate. Add garlic cloves and drizzle garlic-flavored olive oil over each slice. Evenly distribute remaining 1 tbs. olive oil and remaining ingredients around and over cheese rounds. Keep in a cool place until ready to serve.

Makes 8-10 slices

HAM AND RED PEPPER ARAM

Here is a delicious alternative to traditional sandwiches. Find soft cracker bread in the deli or in Middle Eastern markets.

3-4 oz. light cream cheese,
    softened
milk for thinning, as needed
1 large soft cracker bread

2 red bell peppers, roasted, cut
    into strips
5 thin slices Danish ham

In a bowl, thin cream cheese to spreadable consistency with a little milk, if necessary. Spread cheese evenly to edges of bread and top with red pepper strips. Arrange ham slices over bread in 1 or 2 rows so that each portion will have both red peppers and ham. Roll up jelly roll-style in a fairly tight roll. Wrap in pastic wrap until ready to serve. This is easier to cut when cold. Trim ends and cut into 12 equal slices.

Makes 12

PASTRY DOUGH

Use this versatile pastry dough for handpie recipes and for other recipes in this book.

2½ cups all-purpose flour
1 tsp. baking powder
½ tsp. salt

¼ cup olive oil
1 egg
¼ cup white wine or water

Place flour, baking powder and salt in a food processor workbowl and pulse to combine. Add oil, egg and wine. Process until dough is the consistency of sand. Transfer to waxed paper and press particles together to form a ball. Use pastry following recipe directions.

Makes 1 large double crust or 6 handpies

TORTA RUSTICA

A freeform pastry crust encloses a savory spinach, cheese and sausage filling. It travels well and can be baked a day ahead and refrigerated. Bring to room temperature before serving.

1 recipe *Pastry Dough*, page 51
1/2 lb. hot or mild Italian sausages
1 small onion, finely chopped
1/3 lb. small button mushrooms, cut in half or thinly sliced
1 pkg. (10 oz.) frozen chopped spinach, thawed, squeezed very dry
3/4 cup ricotta cheese
1/3 cup diced roasted red bell pepper or pimiento
2 eggs, lightly beaten
6 oz. shredded mozzarella cheese
1/4 cup grated Parmesan cheese
freshly ground pepper
1 egg yolk mixed with 1 tsp. water for egg wash

Make pastry. Roll 1/3 of the dough into a 10-inch circle. Set aside. Roll remaining larger piece of dough into a thicker 12-inch circle and place on a baking sheet lined with parchment paper or foil.

Remove sausage casings and sauté sausage in a medium skillet over medium heat, breaking up meat with a spatula, until fully cooked. Remove with a slotted spoon. Pour out all but 1 tbs. fat. Add onion and mushrooms to skillet and sauté until mushrooms are cooked through, 4 to 5 minutes. Add spinach and cook for 2 to 3 minutes. Remove pan from heat and cool mixture for 10 to 15 minutes. When cool, add remaining filling ingredients and stir well to combine. Heat oven to 375°.

To assemble: Spoon filling over large dough circle to within 1½ inches of dough edges. Center smaller circle over filling. Turn up edges of bottom crust and fold over top crust. Press gently to seal. Cut a small slit in top crust to release steam. Brush crust with egg wash. Bake for 40 to 45 minutes until crust is nicely browned. Remove and cool before serving.

Makes 8 servings

CALZONES

The choice of good things to put into a calzone, first cousin to a pizza, seems endless. Foods to eat out-of-hand are perfect portable fare.

1 recipe *Pastry Dough,* page 51
4 oz. mozzarella cheese, shredded
4 oz. ham or salami, cut into small cubes
1 can (4 oz.) mushroom stems and pieces, drained
1 small onion, thinly sliced
3 tbs. grated Parmesan cheese
½ tsp. dried oregano
½ tsp. dried basil
freshly ground pepper or a few red pepper flakes
olive oil for brushing

Make pastry. Divide dough into 6 pieces. Roll out each piece into a 5- to 6-inch circle. Place mozzarella on half of each circle, leaving a ¾-inch border. Top with meat strips, mushrooms and onion slices. Sprinkle with Parmesan cheese, oregano, basil and pepper. Fold top half of dough over to make a half-moon, pinching dough edges together to seal. Cut a small slit in tops to allow steam to escape.

Heat oven to 375°. Place calzones on a lightly oiled baking sheet. Brush lightly with olive oil and bake until nicely browned, about 25 minutes. Keep in a cool place.

Makes 6

CORNISH PASTIES

Take this version of Cornish miners' traditional lunch on your next picnic.

1 small boiling potato, diced (about ⅔ cup)
1 small carrot, diced (about ⅔ cup)
½ lb. lean ground beef
¼ cup finely chopped onion
1 tbs. minced fresh parsley
1 small clove garlic, finely chopped
salt and freshly ground pepper
1 recipe *Pastry Dough*, page 51
1 egg yolk mixed with 2 tsp. milk

Cook diced potato and carrot in boiling salted water until just tender, 7 to 10 minutes. Drain well in a sieve. In a bowl, mix beef, onion, parsley and garlic. Add potato, carrots, salt and pepper and gently incorporate into meat mixture with your hands.

Heat oven to 350°. Make pastry. Divide pastry into 6 equal pieces. Roll out each piece into a 5-inch circle. Spread 2 to 3 tbs. filling on one half of each dough circle, leaving a 3/4-inch border. Fold top half of each circle over to make a half-moon and seal edges by pressing down with tines of a fork. Place on lightly oiled baking sheet and brush with egg-milk mixture. Cut a small slit in top of each pasty to allow steam to escape. Bake for 45 minutes. Cool on a rack. Keep in a cool place.

Makes 6

VARIATION

Bake standing on the fold to resemble cocks' combs, in keeping with the traditional pasty shape.

PAN-BAGNAT

Countries ringing the Mediterranean make a wonderful stuffed roll or sandwich called pan-bagnat by the French, which translates to "bathed bread." Here is a traditional type of filling for a small hard roll.

DRESSING
1 tbs. full-flavored olive oil
1 small clove garlic, finely
    chopped
1 tsp. red wine vinegar
1/4 tsp. Dijon mustard
freshly ground pepper

FOR EACH SANDWICH
1 freshly baked small roll
prepared olive paste
crumbled feta cheese
pimiento strips
capers
fresh tomato pieces
2 marinated artichoke hearts,
    slivered

Combine dressing ingredients in a small bowl. Cut roll in half, leaving one side hinged. Scoop out most of the soft bread inside. Drizzle dressing generously on both halves. Spread olive paste on both halves and fill with remaining ingredients. Drizzle a little more dressing over filling and close roll, pressing halves firmly together. Wrap tightly in plastic wrap and allow to mellow for 2 hours before eating. Keep cool if sandwich is not going to be eaten in a few hours.

Makes 1

SANDWICH POSSIBILITIES

Sandwiches are great for impromptu picnics. Try these ideas.

- Grilled or broiled eggplant slices, roasted red bell pepper strips, creamy goat cheese and fresh basil leaves on focaccia.

- Thin roasted pork slices with mayonnaise, horseradish and sliced pickled beets on light rye.

- Sliced smoked salmon, capers or cucumbers and cream cheese on rye.

- Fresh goat cheese, olive paste, and roasted red or yellow bell pepper strips on crusty French bread.

- Smoked turkey slices, quartered fresh figs and cream cheese mixed with a blue-veined cheese on walnut bread.

- Cream cheese with chopped peanuts, chutney, roasted chicken slices and a crisp lettuce leaf on whole wheat bread.

- Canned sardines, Monterey Jack cheese and thinly sliced onion rings with mustard on dark rye bread.

- Thin slices of boiled beef brisket, a dollop of prepared Thousand Island dressing and a lettuce leaf or two in a pita pocket.

- A beef salad of finely chopped roast beef, sweet pickles, stone-ground mustard and mayonnaise on whole wheat bread or crisp crackers.

CHOCOLATE BISCOTTI

These are a non-traditional takeoff on the classic Italian cookie.

½ cup unsalted butter, melted
1 cup sugar
1 tsp. vanilla extract
1 tsp. chocolate extract
3 tbs. dark rum or Frangelico liqueur
3 eggs
2½ cups all-purpose flour
3 tbs. cocoa powder
1½ tsp. baking powder
pinch salt
1 cup whole toasted hazelnuts

Heat oven to 350°. In a large bowl, mix butter, sugar, vanilla extract, chocolate extract and rum. Whisk eggs in a small bowl until frothy and stir into butter-sugar mixture. Sift flour, cocoa, baking powder and salt together, add to mixture and stir well to combine. Add hazelnuts and mix well. Form into 2 loaves about 3 inches wide and ¾-inch high on a baking sheet lined with parchment paper. Bake for 20 to 25 minutes until cake-like. The tops of loaves may crack.

Remove from oven and cool for 5 to 10 minutes. Cut loaves into ½-inch slices, return to baking sheet and bake for 10 minutes to crisp. Turn over and crisp the other side for an additional 10 minutes. Remove from oven and cool. Store in an airtight container.

Makes 48

Note: Toast hazelnuts on a rimmed baking sheet in a 350° oven. Shake pan frequently. When nuts start to brown and begin to smell toasty, remove from oven and turn into a rough bath towel on the counter. Rub nuts in towel to loosen skins. Remove as many skins as possible. Cool before adding to cookie dough.

CARROT APPLE CAKE

Grated carrot and apple help keep this moist, flavorful cake fresh-tasting for several days.

1½ cups all-purpose flour
1 tsp. baking powder
½ tsp. baking soda
½ tsp. ground ginger
1 tsp. cinnamon
½ tsp. nutmeg
½ tsp. salt
2 eggs
¾ cup sugar
½ cup vegetable oil
1 tsp. vanilla extract

⅓ cup milk
1 cup finely shredded carrot, about 1 large
1 cup peeled, finely grated apple, about 1 small
½ cup chopped pecans
confectioners' sugar, optional

Heat oven to 350°. Oil and lightly flour an 8-x-8-x-2-inch baking pan. Set aside. Sift together flour, baking powder, soda, ginger, cinnamon, nutmeg and salt. In a bowl, beat eggs until lemon-colored. Add sugar and oil to eggs; beat well. Stir in vanilla, milk and flour mixture. Add carrot, apple and pecans. Pour into prepared baking pan and bake for 35 to 40 minutes, until a toothpick inserted in the center comes out clean. Cool on a wire rack. Dust with confectioners' sugar if desired and cut into squares to serve.

Makes 12-16

JUMBO OATMEAL COOKIES

These large, crisp cookies make a delicious picnic finale.

½ cup butter
½ cup brown sugar, packed
½ cup granulated sugar
1 large egg
1 tsp. vanilla extract
¾ cup all-purpose flour
½ tsp. salt
½ tsp. baking soda
1½ cups quick-cooking oats
⅓ cup chopped walnuts
¼ cup raisins

With an electric mixer, cream together butter and sugars until fluffy. Beat in egg and vanilla. Add remaining ingredients and mix well. Turn dough out on a large piece of waxed paper and form into a roll, about 3 inches in diameter and 8 inches long. Wrap tightly and chill for several hours in refrigerator.

Heat oven to 350°. Remove waxed paper from roll, cut roll into ¼-inch-thick slices and place on an ungreased baking sheet, spacing about 2 inches apart. Bake for 12 to 14 minutes, or until lightly browned and firm to the touch. Cool on a wire rack.

Makes 24

PICNIC BROWNIES

Everyone loves this all-time favorite. Brownies travel well and make a great picnic dessert.

2 squares (1 oz. each) unsweetened chocolate
¾ cup all-purpose flour
½ tsp. baking powder
¼ tsp. salt
½ cup butter
¾ cup brown sugar, packed
2 eggs
1 tsp. vanilla extract
½ cup chopped toasted walnuts
½ cup raisins

Heat oven to 350°. Oil and lightly flour an 8-x-8-x-2-inch baking pan. Set aside.

Melt chocolate squares over hot water or in a microwave. Sift flour, baking powder and salt together. With an electric mixer, beat butter with sugar until well combined. Beat in chocolate, eggs and vanilla. Add flour mixture and stir until just combined; stir in nuts and raisins. Spoon into prepared baking pan and bake for 25 minutes, or until a toothpick inserted in the center comes out clean. Cool on a wire rack. Cut into squares when cool.

Makes 16

JAM TURNOVERS

These jam tarts are easy to make, sturdy enough to travel and satisfy the sweet tooth.

1 recipe *Pastry Dough*, page 51
2 tbs. sugar
1 tbs. water
1/3 cup apricot, strawberry or other fruit jam
1/3 cup chopped pecans or walnuts
1 egg yolk beaten with 1 tsp. water
icing, optional: 1/4 cup sifted confectioners'
sugar mixed with 1 tbs. milk

Heat oven to 375°. Make pastry dough, adding 2 tbs. sugar and 1 tbs. water to dough. Divide and roll out dough into six 5- to 6-inch circles. Place 1 tbs. preserves and a few nuts on half of each circle and spread to within 1 inch of edge. Fold top half over filling to make a half-moon. Seal edges well by pressing down with tines of a fork. Cut a small slit in the top of each tart to allow steam to escape. Place on a lightly oiled baking sheet and brush tops with egg yolk mixture. Bake for 25 minutes, or until nicely browned and firm to the touch. If desired, drizzle icing over tarts while still very warm. Cool on a rack.

Makes 6

VARIATIONS
- **CHERRY OR APPLE TURNOVERS**: Fill each tart with a generous tablespoon of cherry or apple pie filling instead of preserves and nuts.
- **CHEESY FRUIT TURNOVERS**: Spread bottom half of each dough circle with 1 tbs. cream cheese and top with jam or pie filling.

FRESH FRUIT WITH HONEY LIME SAUCE

When melons are at the peak of their season, serve this simple sauce with cantaloupes, honeydews, casabas and Persian melons. The sauce is also good with fresh papaya or peach slices.

grated peel (zest) from 1 lime
1 tbs. honey
1 tbs. lime juice
about 2 cups melon chunks
strawberries, pitted cherries or blueberries for garnish

Combine grated lime peel, honey and lime juice in a small bowl and pour over melon chunks. Keep cold until ready to serve.

Makes 2 servings

FRESH FRUIT WITH
ORANGE YOGURT SAUCE

Tuck this into your cooler and take it along. This is a lovely creamy sauce for fresh fruit, including pineapple chunks, orange slices with seedless grapes, fresh strawberries or peach slices.

2 tbs. vanilla low-fat yogurt
2 tbs. orange juice
2 tsp. honey
2 cup sliced or bite-sized pieces fresh fruit

Combine yogurt, orange juice and honey in a small bowl and pour over fresh fruit.

Makes 2 servings

ELEGANT STRAWBERRIES

Fresh, long-stemmed strawberries make an easy and satisfying dessert to eat with your fingers. Chill the washed strawberries; put the brown sugar and light sour cream in separate little containers for dipping.

8-10 fresh strawberries with stems
2 tbs. light sour cream
2 tbs. brown sugar

Dip each berry into sour cream and then into brown sugar.

Makes 2 servings

CHOCOLATE-DIPPED FRUIT

Fruit dipped in chocolate sauce is a popular dessert.

25-30 fruit pieces: strawberries with stems,
cherries with stems, dried apricots, pineapple chunks,
mango chunks, other favorites
½ cup chocolate ice cream topping
1 tbs. brandy, orange-flavored liqueur or orange juice

Prepare fruit and pack in a covered container. In a medium bowl, stir to combine chocolate ice cream topping and brandy. Cover to pack. To serve, pour the chocolate sauce into small individual bowls and pass the fruit.

Makes 4 servings

INDEX